Requiem

Other Books by the Same Author

———◆———

Verse

LONDON SONNETS

SHYLOCK REASONS WITH
MR. CHESTERTON

KENSINGTON GARDENS

THE UNKNOWN GODDESS

HUMORESQUE

VOLUME IN SIXPENNY SERIES
OF AUGUSTAN POETS

Satire

LAMPOONS

NEWS OF THE DEVIL

Prose

CIRCULAR SAWS

REQUIEM
by Humbert Wolfe

LONDON
Ernest Benn Limited
MCMXXVII

FOR
MY VISITOR
TO A ROOM
ON No. 10
STAIRCASE
AT
WADHAM
COLLEGE,
AND
BECAUSE
OF
EVERYTHING

DEDICATION

THIS is your poem.   I shall not write its fellow
    earthsides of immortality.   I sing
not here, as once, of love and his first swallow
    that does not make, because it is, the spring.

Nor was it written as other poems were
    because of human beauty and brief grace,
that with the bright assurance of a star
    move in the heart to their predestined place,

as smoothly as the moon, and not less argent,
    nor to the sun a hot allegiance lending,
but kindled of themselves with man's insurgent
    claim that the seal of beauty is its ending.

It was not mine to make, but as the pool
    they called Bethesda, when the angel stirred it,
was with some alien virtue wonderful,
    so this was written, as though I overheard it

whispered beyond the misted curtains, screening
    this world from that, so faint and yet so lit
with flame from far, that life itself was leaning
    back, like a runner storming into it.

The moment passed; it is not given to men
    to overtake those echoes with a word.
I am as sure they will not come again,
    as I am certain they were overheard.

But what they were I can no longer guess,
    nor know if anywhere in this a sign
remains of that inhuman loveliness.
    I only know this poem is not mine.

A VERY few of these poems have appeared before. For permission to republish thanks are due to the *New Statesman*, the *Saturday Review*, the *Atlantic Monthly* and the Bermondsey Bookshop.

CONTENTS

THE LOSERS

CONTENTS

THE LOSERS

THE COMMON MAN
I
II

THE COMMON WOMAN
I
II

WHAT WAS life to me, now that I'm done with it?
   (Lucifer, who fell with Adam, and Azrael,
  who took his place in heaven, being lit
  with the dark flames, whose plume is black in Hell,
        Listen and save!
  when that pale spirit calls you from his nameless
    grave.)

On a grey day, when the clouds were thin and long,
   I was born weeping aloud, and she who bore me,
  the innocent malefactor of my great wrong,
  could not relieve my load, nor move the judges for me,
        those who condemn
  men to life's servitude, and none may plead with
    them.

Small wit I had, and the world went wailing by me,
   and youth was a little lantern (Listen and save!
  Lucifer, who fell with Adam!) and love stood nigh
    me,
  but what I had of his wonder I do not have,
        here, all alone,
  unloved, unlit with lamps, forgotten, and unknown.

What could I do but suffer, as all men must,
   and set my mortal heart against the heart of Hell,
  whose soft great beat dissolves our trembling dust,
  as a jar shudders with music (Azrael,
        Listen!) and still
  I matched against the will of death my human will.

I, as the small red insect, dying, builds the dry land
   out of the sea, I, merely by living, laid
   a grain of a grain on that increasing island,
   that not of the heroes, but of us is made,
         who did not dare,
   dying, even to guess that we were dying there.

And proud that island as an Archangel
   rises, when the roaring seas of life are lit
   with the dark flames, whose plume is black in Hell,
   and this was my life, and thus I wrought with it.
         (Listen and tell!
   Lucifer, who fell with Adam, and Azrael!)

THE COMMON MAN

I

I AM the star, that stole the dawn, and died
  with my bright theft, consumed like Semele,
yet in the flame of my burning I denied
  the darkness of God, and men were lit with me.
I am Prometheus, that drew the fiery tide
  of knowledge with the moon of my agony,
but in my chains, and the vulture tearing my side,
  men learned that they must suffer to be free.
Twice have I fallen from heaven, suffered twice
  immeasurable pangs that men may rule
  in unmalicious godhead on the calm hill.
And if the third time I must pay the price
  of the world's torment to be beautiful,
  type of man's unassuageable heart, I will.

II

Who without darkness could imagine light,
    and, were he shadowless, how could the sun
flaunt his gold domino by maskéd night,
    or anything be vivid if all were one!
For those who see, without the need of sight,
    I, Azrael, am the darker stars that spun
about creating God by their own flight,
    giving no radiance, and asking none.
While the lit stars of morning sang together,
    swung out on their own orbit quietly
    my stars, for all their silence, statelier,
and, brightest thou! who plucked the dawn, my brother,
    in the moment of falling from heaven didst not see
    I was the dawn you stole, pale Lucifer!

MY HANDS are empty now at the end of it
   (Lucifer, who fell with Adam, and Azrael,
  who took his place in heaven, being lit
  with the dark flames, whose plume is black in Hell,
      and you, pale Mary,
  see her poor hands how they are spoiled, her feet how
    weary!)

They gave me a little beauty, and a man used it
  as a screen to hide the love he dared not know,
  a love of God, but the love of man confused it,
  a love of children, and I saw them go
      helpless and young
  into the same dim agony with which my heart was
    wrung.

Little I understood, and all I learnt
  was how life passes without hope or warning,
  and to pray for night before the day was burnt,
  and in the night to pray would it were morning,
      and how to seem
  a proud walker in life, when creeping in a dream.

What could I do but suffer, as is the fate
  of women, and as a woman take my share
  in the long litany we dedicate
  to man and to his future that we bear,
      and still pretend
  that that begins for ever, when we end?

(Mary, who, having much, had this more given—
    to build with the pains of birth and the deep Hell
of Death, decreed before the stars, a heaven,
wherein proud Lucifer and prouder Azrael
        at last are one,
    because there is neither life nor death in the Son,

who died that death might be defeated, living
    to make an end of life, you, Ashtaroth,
    and Mary, the greater Queen, are you forgiving
    this common woman, who forgives you both,
        in your high heaven,
    this common woman, who has suffered, and for-
    given?)

My failure was too wan to be disaster,
    too pitiful for tragedy to clothe.
    I listened all my days for love the master
    of life, and in the end was starved of both,
        and yet my will
    that sought, and could not find them, is about them
    still.

I listened for their voice, and was too near them
    in youth, too far in age to hear, and yet
    because I listened other hearts will hear them,
    because I was forgot will not forget,
        because I falter
    the flame, I did not see, burns on the unseen altar.

I

I COULD have made love for them so they basked,
  as children playing in gardens, where the herb
with the lazy lightning of blossom is dusked
  and lit, and there's nothing to hurt or disturb.
Or like Beatrice that Dante only asked
  to stay in his memory, cold and superb,
as when she passed him tall and deeply masked,
  with no heart of her own to ache with, or curb.
But the old dark roots of the tree Ygdrasil
  would have plunged through the flimsy earth, and
    blazed with
  the wild green leafage of irremediable love,
and the hurt they suffered had been more, not less ill,
  when the sleepy soil had been torn, and amazed with
  the floral passion I had not warned them of.

II

ASHTAROTH, you poor goddess, set your doves free !
   Here are new wings and lovelier, since those drew
your car all pearls, and when the laughing sea
   was green as grass in a long avenue.
But now, the deep waters murmur differently,
   since other Feet have blessed them, crying through
the world and all the beaches, " Victory."
   Nor even the lilied wave remembers you.
And Pan, your other shape, (have you not heard ?)
   followed the Kings, piping, to the low manger,
   but the door was shut, and, quiet as a moth,
he stole away.   Nor flock nor shepherd stirred,
   when he, once king of shepherds, now a stranger,
   played the farewell to Pan and Ashtaroth.

Michael! behold night's long black pools are drinking
 the blood-red sun, that through her marshes silts,
 and, though in reddened slime my feet are sinking,
 I lift up the sword of my spirit. Kiss the hilts,
   and say to death,
 "Though you forget my soldier, God remembereth."

For to have fought is better than to have refused
 in a wrong cause, or for no cause at all,
 and, though the blade be shattered, it was used
 in the command of that grey general,
   whose one reward
 to soldiers, having used them, is to break their sword.

(Lucifer, who fell with Adam, and afterward
 through cycle after flaming epicycle
 lead your doomed armies, here is one more sword
 to share that doom, and you, remember, Michael,
   you cannot shame us
 who, failing, cry " te morituri salutamus."

Gladiators, knowing that our agony at most
 is an interlude in some strange festival,
 where the cold spectators watch the chosen ghost
 strive, fall, and die, and then forget it all;
   and yet we come
 shining to the arena, nor beg the lifted thumb.)

What is as foul as war, that changes even
 courage—the soldier's redemption—into lust,
 and smears the very patterns laid up in heaven
 with the crawling inattention of the dust,—
   foul, foul, foul, foul
 great spaces where the winds of futility howl,

25

in darkness, in the decay of all things holy,
   in the broken light of a black star, and still
   the blind rose of the spirit, oh how slowly!
   from age to age sweetens in the secret will,
        as clear of Dis
as over the trenches a storm-cock's litanies.
       Listen!

A THRUSH IN THE TRENCHES

Suddenly he sang across the trenches,
   vivid in the fleeting hush
as a star-shell through the smashed black branches,
   a more than English thrush.

Suddenly he sang, and those who listened
   nor moved nor wondered, but
heard, all bewitched, the sweet unhastened
   crystal Magnificat.

One crouched, a muddied rifle clasping,
   and one a filled grenade,
but little cared they, while he went lisping
   the one clear tune he had.

Paused horror, hate and Hell a moment,
   (you could almost hear the sigh)
and still he sang to them, and so went
   (suddenly) singing by.

Suddenly singing—and thus, out of hate and horror,
   the greater impulse than those that it can move by
shakes itself free, and death becomes a mirror,
   held up by angels, for man to see God's love by,
        and this we were,
   and, thus we challenge you, Michael, says the soldier.

THE SOLDIER

I

Down some cold field in a world unspoken
   the young men are walking together, slim and tall,
and though they laugh to one another, silence is not
      broken:
   there is no sound however clear they call.

They are speaking together of what they loved in vain
      here,
   but the air is too thin to carry the thing they say.
They were young and golden, but they came on pain
      here,
   and their youth is age now, their gold is grey.

Yet their hearts are not changed, and they cry to one
      another,
   " What have they done with the lives we laid aside?
Are they young with our youth, gold with our gold, my
      brother?
   Do they smile in the face of death, because we died?"

Down some cold field in a world uncharted
   the young seek each other with questioning eyes.
They question each other, the young, the golden-
      hearted,
   of the world that they were robbed of in their quiet
      Paradise.

II

I DO not ask God's purpose.   He gave me the sword,
    and though merely to wield it is itself the lie
against the light, at the bidding of my Lord,
    where all the rest bear witness, I'll deny.
And I remember Peter's high reward,
    and say of soldiers, when I hear cocks cry,
" As your dear lives ('twas all you might afford)
    you laid aside, I lay my sainthood by."
There are in heaven other archangels,
    bright friends of God, who build where Michael
        destroys,
    in music, or in beauty, lute-players.
I wield the sword; and, though I ask naught else
    of God, I pray to Him: " But these were boys,
    and died.   Be gentle, God, to soldiers."

THE HARLOT

(LUCIFER, who fell with Adam and Azrael,
   and Mary, who, having much, had this more given—
   to build with the pains of birth and the deep Hell
   of Death, decreed before the stars, a heaven
         are you forgiven,
   dare you forgive this woman, in that high heaven?)

I did not understand.   As in a mist
   dull shapes loomed, threatened, towered over me,
   and passed, while still about me, twist by twist,
   the loose wraiths rolled, too thin to cover me,
         but cold enough
   to strangle all that youth and hope and love are
   fashioned of.

I did not understand.   For my love came to me
   as to the rest, and light and heat and scent with him,
   and in the dusk life spoke his golden name to me,
   and whispered " Follow," and I turned and went
   with him,
         and never knew
   what it was that I did, that others did not do.

I did not understand.   (You, Magdalene,
   rather this head anoint with spikenard
   than His, that all the oil of the world could not wean
   from that which lay before Him, and though 'twere
   hard
         to leave Him, think
   she also has a bitter cup—your cup—to drink.)

I did not understand.   I dreamed that I dreamed
   of kisses that did not kiss, of hands not hands
   but fishes at my throat, and that the world seemed
   like tainted water about deserted lands
         to the dead hum
   of heavy-spotted insects swaying its slow scum.

I did not understand.   Under wan trees
   at night on muted feet dark figures came
   —stale painted lusts, like naked savages—
   that worshipped a pale idol in my name,
         and the dead sea
   stole, as they danced, across the beaches quietly.

I did not understand.   For with the dawn
   the beach was empty, and slowly with the tidal
   drag of the deep the lagging waters were drawn
   into cleanness, and only a broken idol
         lay, still and small,
   watching the unintelligible end of all.

I did not understand.   I once was clean,
   unstained and young, played in a world unbarred,
   and thus was trapped with death.   (You, Magdalene,
   rather this head anoint with spikenard,
         and with your hand
   make smooth the puzzled brow that did not under-
      stand.)

THE HARLOT

I

STRIPED with fierce wales of sunlight the brown idol
   gapes nonchalantly through disfeatured eyes,
while round his trunk bursts in green foam the tidal
   wave of hot creeping plant-obscenities.

He is as blank as those who worship, dumb
   as their dark minds, and does not care, nor know,
when the black chuckle, rubbed across the drum,
   drifts down as palpable as evil snow.

He is the image of their emptiness,
   the carvéd metaphor of minds untaught,
guessing, as we as pitifully guess
   at God, and bringing Him, like us, to naught.

And, while the victim flounders at his knees,
   the nameless god, to whom is sacrificed
the tortured blindness of the savage, sees
   beyond this tumult the slow tears of Christ.

3

II

ALL THE world over in every town and city
    there is a furtive shuffle of tired feet,
and the invisible hounds that know not pity
    pad after them in alley-way and street.
All men are whippers-in of that foul pack,
    and follow them to life's supreme disaster
as certainly as if you heard them crack
    the huntsman's whip, or halloa like the Master.
Their sin is all our sin, ours is their shame,
    and while a single woman earns her bread
by blasphemy committed in love's name
    not only she, but all our world, is dead.
Then God call off the hounds, and bid the whore,
and all who made her, go and sin no more!

THE HUCKSTER

THE WINDS toss up.   Prowling beyond the bar
  smooth-muscled leopards with the foam's white roses
  stippled, the waves are hunting, and no star
  lights the wild jungle, whose green anger closes
            behind and round
  the ship, that into darkness crashes with one bound.

We trade for profit, and if fools pretend
  we waste our lives for gold, what was the quest
  that launched the Argo?   For what other end
  were ever sails set, wearing to the West?
            What other thirst
  than this drew all adventurers from the first?

Say it be true that, when the journey's done,
  we are old men with nothing but our scars
  to show for all the dangers we have run,
  still we have seen the menace of the stars,
            have proved our faith
  with the last testimony of encountered death.

Or if we win great riches, and our touch
  holds before beauty's face the golden mask
  as in the ancient tragedies, this much
  at least of fortune we have dared to ask,
            and have her boon,
  that, if we lived too long, we cannot die too soon.

And if adventure hardens down to theft,
   if the sly huckster creep along the blood
   closing upon the heart, and naught is left
   but pirate-galleys rotting in the mud,
        and for all these pains
   the tattered scarecrows of youth, that dangle on the
      chains,

If, masters of the world, we nothing knew,
   made naught but misery, left naught behind,
   deaf when compassion spoke her shining cue,
   and when love touched our eyelids we were blind,
        if life that cried, as
   a bird, was slowly choked with the gold grain of
      Midas,

Are we to blame? or life the sorceress,
   who with a single potion can pervert
   the desire for action into beastliness,
   the golden shadow into common dirt,
        and blurs the fine
   boundary, that separates the angel from the swine?

(Who of the huckster is the archangel?
   Will none plead for him?   None advance his case?
   Who not with Lucifer from heaven fell,
   nor in the dark of Azrael keeps his place,
        but who would sell
   the angel of light to heaven, of dark to Hell.

Is there no archangel?   No spirit lief
    to lean from heaven and lay his hands on them?
    None? but bright choir was there not a thief
    who had his hour in Jerusalem—
            the thief who won
    [will you give less] upon the Cross his absolution?)

Are we to blame if in Calypso's isle
    our very virtues are to magic bent?
    or if the first long visions that beguile
    the heart of youth become our punishment?
            We are the same
    though thus transformed by devils.   Are we to blame?

I

" TAKE back my thirty pieces
 of silver," the merchant said.
" Now that my wealth increases,
 I would have quiet instead.

" The pieces that you paid me
 I put at interest,
even as my master bade me,
 but quiet is best.

" Another might have spent it
 on pleasure, wine or maid.
I only used or lent it
 all in the way of trade.

" But now, that I fail and tire,
 I see my duty plain;
I have but one desire,
 to give it back again.

" You tell me it was bartered
 for a soul, and you decline?
But if a soul was martyred,
 high priest, the soul was mine.

" My soul it was I offered,
 my heart it was I paid,
and I it was who suffered,
 myself who was betrayed.

" You are the priests.   The stuff is
      there in the temple!   So,
   since comfort is your office,
      take it, and let me go.

" Take it—for if I erred then,
      have you not also erred?
   and if I spoke a word then,
      who bade me speak the word?

" You are the priests.   Forgive me!
      I know not what I do.
   Nay, tell your men to leave me!
      and listen! this is true—

" Last night I saw a felon
      hanging, his face all black
   with birds, and one great talon—
      For God's sake take it back! "

II

THERE were thirteen that ate together, drinking
  strange wine, and biting on a perilous bread.
And one was speaking, and the rest were thinking
  more of his eyes than of the things he said.
They were dark eyes, and in their deep was swaying
  a mote of gold, that lit upon the word
subtly, as though the light in them were saying
  what, though unspoken, all, who listened, heard.
Most willingly they were caught in the gold strand
  that bound their hearts only to set them free,
save one, who heard, but would not understand,
  afraid of blindness, if he dared to see.
But even so there was a ray of light
went out with him into the fatal night.

THE NUN

THERE is a pool in the convent garden.   Still is
   the amber basin, where no fishes leap,
   but slowly cruise between the water-lilies
   in sleepy gold, as those in silver sleep—
          sleep on and on,
   their sleep itself a quiet breathing orison.

In spring, like four tall monks, the cypresses
   fold their dark green about their cloistral boughs,
   while the young birches, those most human trees,
   so sheltered, take their first and silver vows,
          and flowers swing
   their coloured censers in fragrance softly opening.

There is small noise of wind behind these walls,
   nor any human echo save bells sobbing,
   whose normal cadence actually falls
   upon the pool, and sets the water throbbing
          with the far sense
   of some angelic trouble, some healing difference.

Pool of my heart!   Not always was thy cup
   guarded from the wind as now, as now unstirred,
   nor did the water-flowers drifting up
   spread their green plumage like a floating bird,
          nor naught disturb
   with any flash of fin the lilies' trailing herb.

But passion deeply moving, loss and terror,
   anger and sorrow, turpitude and blame,

41

changed all, and what was made to be a mirror
  for unassuming loveliness became
      of shapes, that pass
in dark, a broken and tumultuous looking-glass.

Thus tarnishing with rust the silent mere
  beyond the world, whose stainless waters draw
  from the small pools the saints establish here
  in passionless obedience to the law,
      that says " Refuse!
What we denied remains, but what we had we lose."

(Dear Saint Teresa! who laid the world aside
  before the world had spoken, will you bless
  after such pain this all-but-virgin bride
  of Christ, who will not be His lover less
      because she shared
the enchanting agony of love, that you were spared?

Will you not take her softly by the hand,
  nor tell her that she sacrificed in vain
  for music, that she did not understand,
  the lovely human counterpoint of pain,
      whose echoes faint
are grace-notes in the full acceptance of the saint?)

It is very quiet in the garden. Slowly
  the oleanders let their roses fold.
  The shadows reach my feet, and all the holy
  precincts of evening are suddenly cold.
      Sweet Christ! a nun
lies down to sleep, and for the last time rejects the
  sun.

THE NUN

I

IN THE garden of my Father
    there is a lilac-tree,
and the fowls of heaven gather
    from all the world for me,

the quail He sent to Moses,
    Elijah's ravens, and,
all white between the roses,
    in worship's Holy Land,

when the lilac-tree is bending
    beneath the weight of love,
I have heard wings descending,
    but dared not see the Dove.

I will walk alone in the Garden
    in which my soul has cried,
"God! if you cannot pardon
    the world I laid aside,

and if by having strayed there,
    and loved it, while I strayed,
My Master was betrayed there,
    I also was betrayed."

And, while the fowls of heaven
    between the branches gather,
though I am unforgiven
    I will whisper to my Father:

" Last night, when I was waking,
    I saw the bitter Rood,
and One upon it breaking
    His heart in solitude.

" Dear God, my heart was shaken,
    and in the utter black
I heard Him cry ' Forsaken '—
    For Christ's sake take me back."

THE NUN

II

OUTSIDE the corn is unto harvest yellow,
   outside the first blue clusters change the vine,
but in this reticence my heart lies fallow,
   waiting for other bread, and holier wine.
My soil is barren, but with fasting and sorrow
   enriched I will prepare it for the plough,
knowing the shares can only drive the furrow
   deeply and straight if I am patient now.
I will refuse to share life's easy rain
   that falls alike on evil and on good.
I will deny the sun's diurnal stain
   on truth's immaculate beatitude.
And I shall know that love and all delight
are silver tares the moon has sown by night.

THE ANARCHIST

SALUTE to Nature, the first anarchist,
   whose bombs of green explode the fertile spring,
   and hurl the heats of summer with a twist
   like poison-gas that, slowly filtering,
       on shred and splinter
   of the bombarded lines of autumn clamps the
     winter.

She has no law, but wastes the myriad spawn
   to hatch a single fish, in grim bravado
   builds trees whose emerald lace by time is drawn
   into secular beauty, and with one tornado
       crashes and sears
   the intolerable patience of the designing years.

She has one impulse only—to create
   in order to destroy in wilfulness,
   and if she has a secret, it is hate
   of all the cringing armaments of " yes "
       that scatter and blow
   at the careless onset of her eternal " no."

That is the freedom I demand for man—
   no king, no law, no guide, no love, no God,
   life with no purpose, death that has no plan,
   contempt the axe, and nescience the rod
       with which we crack
   out of life's black oppression into further black.

We shall not be deceived if we forestall
   the laughter of the uncreated rabble,
   who mock us with the phantom of the Fall,
   the ghost of resurrection, and the bright babble
      of man restored
   by his own guess at some fear-generated Lord.

(You to whom men in Athens sacrificed—
   the Unknown God, because unknowable,
   —an older Mithras and a darker Christ—
   release these disenchanted from the spell,
      who cannot be
   comforted by all imagination's wizardry.

Give them enchantment. Let them know again
   the puzzled happiness of blindness humbled,
   and let them cry like your Athenians, when
   Paul broke the altar, and the statue tumbled,
      " Though thus deceived,
   blessed are we who did not know, yet have not
    disbelieved.")

We will be ourselves, and when the devil in us
   cries loudly " I am God," we shall reply,
   " There is no God, save your own voice within us,
   the tired echo of death that, drifting by,
      pauses to write
   with ultimate indifference, ' Let there be night.' "

THE ANARCHIST

I

Yes, poppies, I understand your red.
  You are protesting against death and dulness.
You are shouting (and they hear not), "Dead, dead,
    dead,"
  in a huge unsensitive stillness.

The black earth and the dull black people
  are no more than meaningless substantives,
a worn lesson-book for a blind cripple,
  but your colour is clear print and it lives.

Red caps of liberty among slaves,
  wild daughters of the revolution,
your flag of crimson suddenly waves
  over the Bastille of nation after nation.

You are crying aloud to us, "Anguish and freedom,"
  and there are not ten just men found to heed you.
You are fire from heaven falling on Sodom!
  Burn all the cities of the world, poppies! They need
    you.

II

BUT I will not be cheated of freedom.   No!
　　I will walk along the black and barren street,
and see the small distorted people go,
　　and hear how thin a city's heart can beat.
I will justify destruction by the pains
　　all men are born to suffer.   I will prove
that of all life's intolerable chains
　　the last that man must shatter will be love.
I will plumb the deepest Hell that man has known,
　　and find in agony the perfect hater,
who proudly claims damnation for his own,
　　and uses it to damn his dark Creator,
and watch creation choking in the mist
　　of God, the universal anarchist.

THE RESPECTABLE WOMAN

IT SHOULD have been easy to die moderately,
  having lived without excess. To escape the extreme
  experience of Death's command to see,
  beyond these modified tones, the single beam
      whose flagrant knife
  slashes into aching fragments the pattern of life.

What was my pattern? If I worked in wool
  the crimson silks of vision, love's gold lace,
  subduing what was strange and beautiful
  to the grey shadow of my stooping face,
      yet none the less
  that was the steady shadow cast by godliness.

Is there no virtue in bearing down the threat
  of the jungle moving faintly in the blood,
  and the smooth velvet footsteps, and the wet
  muzzles of creatures, stirring in the mud,
      and the hot breath
  that men called freedom to live, and I called death?

There were high names, but I was not deceived.
  I saw the beast beneath the shifting cloak.
  Was I not blessed, who saw and disbelieved,
  who, when all else went singing, never spoke,
      but shut my eyes
  against the baits of knowledge and freedom's glitter-
    ing lies?

Women there were who sinned, and these I turned
    from,
  and men who claimed to set creation free
  by changing all the laws that men have learned from
  God and their own unchanging history,
        women and men
  who were the devil, leading back his own again.

They came with music, and with roses, trailing
  their beautiful damnation, and the victim
  that listened woke to find the rapture failing
  in the flushed instant, when its beauty tricked him,
        but I, who saw
  the cloven hoof of loveliness, upheld the law.

I stood for unflinching ignorance, and man's duty
  to do in darkness God's obscure command,
  and thrusting by intelligible beauty
  I followed what I could not understand,
        because I knew
  that that alone which passes understanding must be
    true.

(Martha! who found in service the better part,
  these are your sisters. These, like you, preferred
  hearing the little whisper of the heart,
  some colder admonition that they heard,
        and sacrificed
  for that bleak satisfaction, even Christ.

54

And, therefore, Martha, since they too were jealous
   of love rewarded by the Source of love,
   is there no word He spoke that you can tell us,
   or even an unrecorded smile to prove
       they shall not starve
   in heaven, on earth who only stand and serve?)

But death comes suddenly with a great wind,
   stripping the spirit naked to the light,
   and I must suffer not less than those who sinned
   the exposure that I gave my life to fight,
       and yet I know
   I did not err, though God Himself should tell me so.

I

THEY are singing, but I have not listened
  in the open spaces in spring.
Their white feet in the dances have hastened,
  but mine are not hastening.

They have loosed their hair that is golder
  than laburnum's gold in May,
and the birch in the rain is their shoulder—
  but I have looked away.

They have bound their breasts with rushes,
  they have dived in the forest lake,
but the foot of the satyr crushes
  the lilied reeds in the brake.

The sound of a flute drifts over,
  (but I have closed my ears)
and the air is sweet with the lover,
  and the cry of the fugitive years.

I have not heard nor seen them,
  I have not danced nor sung,
and when love passed between them
  he left my heart unwrung.

They have wasted their lives by spending,
  and are with death rewarded,
but I shall find no ending
  of the life that I have hoarded.

I saved the source of living,
    Thou knowest at what cost,
and, therefore, All-forgiving,
    now give me what I lost !

II

IT IS a common lie—who would believe it?—
  that, as men lose their beauty, the slow earth
does in her tranquil motherhood re-weave it
  into a bird—into a flower-birth.
It is not true.   The earth has no such power.
  But spring to spring is hostile; summer saith,
"Was there another summer?"; bird and flower
  have nothing half so lovely as their death.
And if men say no drop in rapture's cup
  but is some beauty known, and re-engendered
  now, as hereafter, for the millionth time,
remember lost Atlantis silted up,
  and crawling seas between the beauties squandered
  of gods face downwards in the ocean slime.

THE WINNERS

HE

Thus it began. On a cool and whispering eve,
   when there was quiet in my heart, she came,
   and there was an end of quiet. I believe
   that a star trembled when she breathed my name,
           and, when I spoke,
   not in our East ascending, a dawn broke.

There was a colour beyond the mortal prism,
   a light, with darkness, as its minor third,
   fragrance, as though an everlasting chrism
   too subtle for sense, were spoken in a word,
           not in our speech,
   but colour, light and fragrance answering each to
     each.

(Lucifer, who fell with Adam and Azrael,
   Mary, who, having much, had this more given,
   Michael and Mary Magdalene, if Hell
   saw some bronze dawn the parapets of heavens,
           intolerably far,
   and bright, and unattainable, so love's one star,

seen from the abyss of smoking life, and you
   Krishna, or Balder, or some older name
   for the unimaginable beauty breaking through
   the tossing veils of vision, this is the same
           beauty that died,
   and rose again, when the world's heart was crucified.)

5   63

Say that love passes, crying in a mist,
   say that I failed her, say that, being this,
   even at the high moment of love's Eucharist
   I bartered my starry birthright for a kiss,
        and when she bent
  her bright and serving head, betrayed her sacrament.

Yet she forgave me, yet with the star she strove,
   saying, " Dear star, rather than he should blame
   his treason, I will fashion with my love
   some lesser star, and call it by your name,
        and, though I lose you,
  if there must be a choice, dear star, I cannot choose
   you."

So she stepped down, out of her natal splendour,
   to comfort me, and saw the great light dwindle,
   but, at the dark horizons of surrender,
   now, at the end, I see the star rekindle,
        and, dying, know
  there was no star but she, nor will be, where I go.

THE LOVERS

HE

I

ROMANCE? Has she escaped? But, wait!
  Surely that goat-boy heard
a step as undeliberate
  and swift, as the low word

spoken by the beloved, and, wheeling
  suddenly to the height,
he watched illumination stealing
  the very source of sight.

Look at his eyes. They do not heed us,
  enchanted and forsaken,
but their bright misery may lead us
  upon the path that she has taken.

She touched his eyelids with a morning
  that left him beautiful and blind
to be a promise, and a warning
  of what we too may find.

So into noon between the firs
  climb where no shadow moves,
and learn that the forest-lawns are hers
  (but their silences are love's).

Climb on! (and does he watch in twilight
  the goatherd, where he lies,
the actual stars mislead the shy light
  abandoned in his eyes?)

Climb on, and find a mountain-inn,
   and, while he sleeps, the noise
of rain on the roof is a violin
   quietly tuned to your voice.

Your voice, in which day's shadows creep
   warm, perfumed, intimate
with drowsy words that fall asleep
   of their own weight.

And, last of all, when you are sinking
   into quiet, and only your eyes
glimmer, like that lost torch-boy linking
   his unknown Paradise,

and you stretch your negligent fingers, wooing
   beauty into her trance,
then all our life, that was vainly pursuing,
   like his, becomes romance.

HE

II

No! do not speak!   It is better to stand so
  in air as palpable as water about us
with lips close-shut lest it should drown us.   No!
  we need not speak, since this had never been without
    us.

It is your hand in mine that has lit the lake,
  a bowl with a lamp shining through alabaster,
a bowl some Ganymede has lifted to slake
  the thirst divine of his tall white mountain-master.

It is your still gold head, in the wave of the wind
  like a Naiad's head, that makes the great mountains
    dress
their spears at the salute.   A thought in your mind
  tumbled on the autumn trees their sunset loveliness.

It is because you stand remote above
  the beauty of the world you are making, slender
as the slim reed at the young lips of love,
  that Time has broken his sword and the years
    surrender.

It is because you have leaned a little toward me,
  not as a lover, but as the holier part
of the poet's mind, that this fugitive ecstasy
  outpaces even what the heart can say to the heart.

For love has but two notes, and those notes shake
  beyond themselves from the heard to the unheard
    note,
and so fall back.   And in dark the lovers wake,
  but we shall not wake in dark, for this is the third
    note.

HE

III

I AM the fiddler.   Ere the world began
   I had two notes, and only two.   The one
with tumbled sunflakes dripping, I called man,
   the second had no name and needed none.
I am the fiddler.   Like a golden fan
   I folded the long feathers I had spun,
and, as I folded them, a shadow ran,
   silver, between the music and the sun.
I threw my bow over the stars, and no man
   remembered Krishna, but, till the world is done,
   there are but these two notes, a single tune,—
man, that I named before the world, and woman,
   so named when she redeemed the fallen sun
   with the vicarious silver of the moon.

SHE

LISTEN! The world was quiet when he came,
    and the clear moon, turning to glass the air,
    could hardly pierce it with her argent flame,
    but hung, in cool suspension, mirrored there,
        but when he spoke
    the glass of the moon was in his voice, and the glass
    broke.

Broke—and some splinter cut away the net,
    in which a singing lark had been snared, and she,
    afraid of her own wings, would not rise yet,
    but hid in my heart a moment, swayingly,
        while far above
    there was a high star drew this little star to love—

love in his moment, that does not ask or give,
    love in his moment uncompassionate,
    love, that is a death, in which the lovers live
    between the mortal and the immortal state,
        than death no less
    love that knows unimaginable loneliness.

And still she hid—my lark—(and who can tell
    what is the lovely threat and terror of wings
    for all who fly?) but, suddenly, she fell
    clean into heaven out of all these things,
        and as she tumbled
    the long beam of her singing in the moonlight
    trembled.

(Psyche, do you remember the wings beating,
    and all the little earth that fell so far,
    when you, all wingless, through the midnight fleeting,
    woke among wings upon an alien star,
            unknown, untrod,
    and, turning to your lover, knew him for a god?

Psyche, if you remember this, remember
    how long the first flight is, the woman how waking,
    in what wild world unguessed, after what slumber,
    with the heart crying and the wings how aching,
            remember these
    lonely, between the kisses, and love's long silences

And then remember how through all sorrow after,
    weeping, and the slow mitigation of the flight,
    still some clear echo of the lark's high laughter
    sounds, and wings beating upward through the night,
            upward and out
    to where the straight trumpets are calling, and the
        gold stars shout.)

I chose between my soul and him—no choice
    since he became my soul, and, dying, know
    that, though all voices fade in love's one voice,
    and all but this are silent where I go,
            the path I trod,
    alone, was lonely with the loneliness of God.

SHE

I

YES, THEY will give me there
 all that I missed here.
Ah! but I shall not know
 lips that I kissed here.
Coldly the harp of silver,
 coldly, how cold,
the harpist will stroke the great
 harp of gold—
cool, grave, immaculate
 notes, but how graver
than life's small cadences
 hushed there for ever,
how in their absolute
 counterpoint less to me
than love's voice breaking on
 his fugitive " Yes " to me,
than love's voice changing from
 a sob to a dumb thing,
but in the silences
 plucking on something
the shade of things mortal, a
 butterfly's trace on
God's inconceivable
 diapason.

THE LOVERS

SHE

II

I WAS not envious of beauty in your verse,
  save when your own, being mortal, fell below it,
nor asked Euterpe aught of what was hers,
  save when she robbed the man to crown the poet.

Ah! I was proud as she when with a mouthful
  of words you changed men's hearts, and with a tune
turned the dull North of hatreds into a South full
  of love, and the first nightingale beneath the moon.

Ah! I was proud as she, where silence lay dense
  as mist on all those waiting for the spring
in the hollow centuries, when your bright cadence
  flashed like a torch, like a gold swallow's wing.

Ah! I was proud, but what you did for these
  the living, and the unborn, could you not do
for yourself also? bring that shining peace
  to your wild heart? not save your own love too?

O dear vicarious lover, with your head bowed,
  holding the crown high above foreheads unknown,
sealing their love and peace, ah! I was proud,
  prouder than Euterpe, poet—and alone.

SHE

III

THE GREAT Italian made his statues wear
   the rhythm of his mind as absolute
as though he poured the metal like an air
   along the cool obedience of a flute.
And yet when all was finished, on the smooth
   of bronze or marble side some alien glow
descended with the menace of a truth,
   that baffled even Michael Angelo.
So love, though shaped to follow perfectly
   the ultimate vision men and women spend
for that brief peace at the flame's heart, goes free
   by some strange light their passion could not lend.
Love is greater than the lovers.   Love is such
   that all may love, and fail, and yet be rich.

THE BUILDER

SPACE is a thin black fog that coils and smokes
   with long loose-lipped defiance, but we pack it
   into the stuff of vision, whose golden strokes
   tear at the formless void until they crack it,
       and in the brain
   burst into pattern's unimaginable pain.

Arches thrust out like the back of a maddened horse,
   braced as with striving hoofs at emptiness,
   the lunge of the sheer stone with the white force
   of fire pouring upward into space,
       the meteor shower
   in traceries transfixed, and the unquestionable
   tower.

Or blocks, head-downwards into rivers stamped,
   drowned in the mud and holding, though they drown,
   while on their suffocating valiance clamped
   vast girders leap, so that you feel the frown
       of frozen flight,
   and almost hear the groan of wings that fail to bite.

There is one splendour of vision, another glory,
   different and less, of the vision consummate
   snatched from the void in steeple and clerestory
   and the tall iron irresolutely great,
       the builder's tale
   of all the strivings of men that thus divinely fail.

(Lucifer, that fell from heaven, and Azrael—
  space in triumphant darkness—you were lit
even with the burning of pinions as they fell,
each bound for ever to his opposite—
        type of man's soul
divided thus for ever, thus for ever whole.

And though you fell, pale angel, it is thus
  you hung the unappeasable stars to mark
the long way back that climbs for all of us
untrodden and enchanted through the dark,
        and all our pride
is that the desire of the heart is never satisfied.)

The desire remains.   So let the builder go,
  whose work is only to kindle it anew.
The desire remains for beauty they did not know,
they failed and builded better than they knew,
        who failing wind
the secret slug-horn at the ramparts of the mind.

Childe Rolande is at the gate.   The paynim gloom
  grapples his throat, but still he sounds again
man's last rejoinder that, outfacing doom,
  awakes the startled hosts of Charlemagne
        crying in the night
  "The heathen dark has wrong, Christians have
  right."

THE BUILDER

I

THEORIES of Art! Believe me, they're no theories!
To know yourself, to clutch what now and here is
and set it down for yourself—that's all there is
in all that chatter about mysteries!
Take my Gioconda (Mind! the paint is wet,
And stand well back! She isn't finished yet!)
What made me paint her just like that, d'you think?
Shade, line and colour! Fools to waste their ink!
All that is in it—that's the stuff of the trade,
as a man of bone and flesh is moulded and made.
Yes, but does God stop there? Does He design
this as an exercise in colour and line
and rest content with that? And dust His thumb
as though He'd finished working out a sum!
In His own image He makes us—meaning He
creates each soul with separate agony,
tearing it out of His own—and using flesh
(as I, as anyone, might use his brush)
to set His mind free of a thought that stung Him
into creation. What d'you say? I wrong Him
to speak of Him in human terms. How else
can we speak of Him? Of all miracles
the greatest is that a man understands
God in the godhead of his shaping hands
when he moves them blindly, when he gropes, he grips,
and the thrill of life cracks through his finger-tips.
So let's get back to God. It is not enough
for Him to be. The wild star-radiant stuff
of what He is struggles, is wracked, is torn
like a harp bursting—and a world is born.
Does He in the agony of birth, on the rack
of that adorable suffering stand back
and murmur, " Value, colour, balance, line,"

6

or when the dawn-gold spur of an Apennine
cleaves chaos, like a sword, red with His blood,
sob to the morning-stars as they sing " It is good "?
Then look at my Gioconda!   See how she pinches
her cold clear lips, and count my soul by inches
creeping from corner to corner of her mouth and so
to the cheek, to the eyes, to the hair, and watch it grow
not into a face, (for that were only a trick
of neat additional arithmetic)
but into Leonardo himself, and the life she pinches
between her lips is the life that is Da Vinci's.

That's what Art is—and now enough of talk.
Give me my brush, friend, and that powdered chalk.

II

FOR IN this we are justified—
　to set down what we have seen,
and strange voices have cried
　strange words between

saying " Beauty," saying " Love,"
　not as we know or say them,
and the shadows we are made of
　vex and bewray them.

But, like men stemming a crowd,
　we hold back the press,
and a little space is allowed
　to this loveliness,

that is not ours, nor anyone's,
　but in whose service we
make smooth the path that runs
　from the sea to the sea.

III

COME! let us write our mortal signature
   across the unsubjective world, and claim
that all its temporal attributes endure,
   and some are beautiful, because we came.
Or say the moon did never evening lure
   with her cold magic till we spoke her name,
nor the great star of the sun was ever sure,
   till we saluted him, of his tall flame.
Let us endow the universe, and feel it
   slide through the wavering borderlands of sense,
and in the instant of creation seal it
   with thought's sign-manual of permanence.
So God, when He had fashioned them, would sign
   His Dents du Midi or an Apennine.

I ALSO build, but not with steel nor stone,
    but with the shadowy bricks of innocence,
    and mortar that the heart has made her own,
    and what I build has neither roof nor fence
           that can deflect,
    with limits or an end, the visionary architect.

This is more than the upward anguish of the spire,
    more than the vaulting bridge, that all but flies :
    it is the consecration, and the fire
    fallen from far : it is the voice that cries,
          " Make the way smooth
    for the feet of the lord of the world, whose name is
      youth."

He comes out of the hills from a small town.
    He has the sun in his hair and his eyes are lit,
    and the thorns of the world are blossoms for his
      crown,
    and I am she who crowns his head with it.
          Yes! I have found him
    lost in the desert of his heart, and crowned him.

I crown him and I go, but he is hurled
    into life's beauty against the plausible gods
    of sleek content, and master of the world
    establishes his starry periods,
          and in his turn
    passes, but because of him the living gods return.

Return, and he is lost to me, who freed him,
   as I was lost to him, when he was freed,
   but since the world will then no longer need him,
   I also will absolve him of my need,
       when that is done
   for which the God in me sent forth his well-belovéd
   Son.

(Mary, who, having much, had this more given,
   who in the dark when all your pains were done
   knew that your babe was in Himself the heaven
   for which all other women lose their son,
       nor they alone,
   Mary, who make the future out of their blood and
   bone.

They make a Saviour, and no Angels hail him.
   No gain of all the world consoles their loss.
   They set his eyes toward the light, and fail him
   because they cannot modify his Cross,
       set at the dim
   end of the path they traced, but cannot walk with
   him.)

And yet without my building all were vain.
   The airy towers and the terraced slope
   of cities are the birthright of my pain,
   and the dream I lost and my abandoned hope,
       by vision fanned,
   are the torch that the runners pass from hand to
   hand.

THE TEACHER

I

THIS I believe:
that if I do not will
the Universe stands still.
I and those of whom I am the part
built it and changed it in our heart,
not out of mud, nor stone, nor seas,
but out of that in which all these
begin, are all, and naught—
the deep desiring thought.

This I believe:
The ape
of which I wear the shape
tumbled in me—his Hell—
a furry archangel,
and, with the only skill he had,
swung with one pitiful blackpad
into the jungle of my will
desiring, till
with a final stroke
he tore his prison-vesture off, and spoke.
He threw aside, because he willed,
the coat that clamped and killed,
and shall he not assume, if he have striven,
when all is done, investiture in heaven?

This I believe:
I am the ape
that God made in His shape,
and who, when he has changed all this,
will at the last refashion God in his.

II

THEY murmur, the children, like bees in summer
  in a hot garden, like bees in a cup,
and, like light through branches, now gay, now dimmer,
  thought touches a face that is lifted up.
My bees, with the pollen under your feet,
  when the thought we shared is no longer alive,
will aught that we dreamed of together be sweet,
  will there be honey of ours in the hive?
It is dark in the hive.   There is fear, there is shame,
  there are tears, and ugliness unto death.
Sweet thieves of the sun, must it still be the same,
  or will not the flowers you rifled bequeathe
a glimpse of the vision you saw at my knees,
when the teacher was taught by the Keeper of Bees?

THE SAINT

HE

SAINT FRANCIS of Assisi, do you remember
  the sacred mountain, green above the lake,
  where first the vines and then the olives clamber,
  and the flowers, so lulled with beauty, never wake—
        gold, crimson, blue,
  on the long drowsy terraces you loved and knew?

Still in the lake the painted island-town
  to the brown shelter of its Minster creeps,
  and still the kerchiefed boatman, bending down,
  scarce stirs the burnished water with his sweeps,
        and from the hill
  the monastery bells affirm your gospel still.

Your gospel of the birds and of the flowers,
  how every petal God has deigned to paint
  has by its mere enamel all the powers,
  and more than all the beauty of the saint,
        and how the swallow
  worships with arrow flight that prayer is feign to
  follow.

Your gospel of acceptance, that transposes
  God, and this earthly beauty He has made,
  finding the resurrection in the roses
  and all the angels in a single blade,
        and having heard
  the Twelve Apostles in the voice of a bird.

And, as with beauty, so with ugliness
　　asking the mire, that your feet had trod,
　　with its long patience to redeem and bless
　　the soul's impatience, when the feet of God
　　　　　　pass by, as though
　　He cared not what He crushed, and did not even
　　know.

With ugliness, or what so seemed, and sin
　　that is no more than beauty's other side,
　　your gospel, like your Master, entered in
　　and by acceptance proved, what sin denied,
　　　　　　that wickedness
　　is part of the soul of God, and calls to Him no less.

You sought no cloister, but with their wild-rose fire
　　you built of understanding and of pardon
　　the walls, that shut out envy, hate, desire,
　　or changed them into flowers in your garden,
　　　　　　since all were part
　　of the burden of man, and therefore of your heart.

Still in your sacred mountain the cold lances
　　of the moon ring the target of your mere,
　　and while one man loves birds and flowers,
　　　St. Francis,
　　you and the company of saints are here,
　　　　　　while one man knows
　　that all creation is simple as a rose,

fades like a rose, and has the rose's thorn,
but sees behind the fallen petal the bud,
and understands, although his heart is torn,
there was and is salvation in blood,
while anyone
lies down to sleep, accepting everything beneath the
sun.

HE

I

THESE are not flowers.   They are Adam seeing
    the grasses in the empty Garden weave
out of their love the many-coloured being
    in which they trembled at the feet of Eve.

These are not flowers.   They are Moses breaking
    the sullen rock in the desert with his hand.
They are, spring-cooled, the vision re-awaking
    of the green pastures in the Promised Land.

These are not flowers.   They are Jacob waiting
    for Rachel seven years, and, when she came,
finding that April had been hesitating
    for seven years to justify her name.

These are not flowers.   They are David crying,
    " Absalom, Absalom, O, my son, my son! "
They are the echoes down the years replying,
    " Absalom, Absalom," softly on and on.

These are not flowers.   They are Mary hearing
    the promise of the Saviour and His burden.
They are not flowers, but a woman bearing
    the rose of heaven in an earthly garden.

These are not flowers.   They are God renewing
    the Eden that His Adam sacrificed.
They are not flowers.   They are heaven wooing
    man with the floral benison of Christ.

HE

II

WHERE in the mountains in their shining ranks
    the flowers march, it is easy to believe
in the God of flowers, and to give Him thanks
    Who wears His floral heart upon His sleeve.
Here, where is harbourage for butterflies,
    perfectly matching flowers shade by shade,
till wings appear to sink, and blossoms to rise,
    it would be strange if a man had not prayed.
It would be strange here where the bees discover
    the pollen that enriches giver and taker,
if man the loved should not accept the Lover,
    or in the moment of making refuse the Maker.
And if a flower in her cup can hold Him,
    is there not room in the heart of man to fold Him?

SHE

Do YOU remember, Joan, (O vain to wonder
　if you remember how the evening star,
　a thousand times you drove the herd home under,
　admitted you to vision's Calendar,
　　　　like any child
　by that tall friendship, and the quiet moon beguiled?)

Do you remember the Dom Rémy you knew,
　the plain and the small mountain-range of ricks,
　the poplars at their goose-step, two by two,
　the brown hen-church that folded her stone-chicks,
　　　　your father's farm
　so dear, so small it almost fitted in your arm?

Do you remember (even through the flame)
　after the long day's labour in the field
　how with the Angelus you heard your name
　mixed with the bells, and hid your face and kneeled
　　　　when sweet and high
　a peasant heard " ecce ancilla Domini "?

" Behold the servant of the Lord—and France,"
　and in your hands, that never held a sword,
　the country staff was lifted like a lance
　in the hushed aisles of evening, to the Lord,
　　　　and you were gone
　for ever, Joan, to put immortal iron on.

94

What was your sainthood, Joan? You did not guess
    when you restored his lilies to your king
    that you had found beyond the fleur-de-lys
    the lilies in an everlasting spring
            whose wind is blown
    across the centuries, and is fragrant, Joan.

You were not a proud saint. You went alone
    among the soldiers, and you understood
    how men are only frightened angels, Joan,
    and evil only unprotected good;
            you knew these things,
    and knew how pardonable are the hearts of kings.

And, being a woman, you lifted mankind up
    against the devil in their own despite,
    and when they feared, you drank the bitter cup
    for all your cowards as by woman's right,
            and, even when
    you burned, you did not blame them, knowing they
        were men.

Saint Joan, it may be all things human must
    be dull with earth, and with the darkness saint,
    but if it be so, then your mortal dust
    was purged with flame till you were all a saint,
            and when you prayed
    fire spoke to fire, and mixed in heaven, Maid.

SHE

I

THERE is no need to bind the lilies:
    she has laid them to her breast.
She has gathered the flowers.   As her Father's will
    is
    let us leave her.   It is best.

They will not fade where she has set them.
    They will not fade and, though
France and the cause she died for should forget
    them,
God will remember.   Let us go

THE SAINT

SHE

II

AND THE massed English soldiery stood by,
  an army of the damned by a devil painted—
steel cap and jerkin—with the crimson dye
  of their Hell-fire, in which the Maid was sainted.
So all men with a faggot or a trick
  burn the hot vision of youth, and watching it rise
to heaven, are varnished by their heretic
  with the great gold of transitory surprise.
But afterwards glows there a single ember,
  in the pale inch by its wan candle lit
they find their youth reflected, and remember
  how once the world and heaven blazed with it.
And, though nor youth nor vision will return,
  with their bright death, the hearts, that burned them,
    burn.

GREATNESS? But by what measure do you mete—
  By what I did, or what I sought and lost,
  by the hot whisper of the roaring street,
  or the cold lips of the unapproving ghost,
        that slides between
  the little thing I am and what I might have been?

There have been men that have surpassed their fate,
  finding a star in the mud. These in the things
  they could have had and left unclaimed were great,
  these in the kingdoms they refused were kings.
        These, plunging deep
  into the dreams' bright origins, found dreams to keep.

Vision! as snowflakes, silver in the night,
  stain the dark air, or a star's coloured dust
  paints the pale heavens with the source of light,
  so vision, beauty's unassuageable lust
        for the unattained,
  abides with the chosen, gold, as a star had stained.

And greatness is the vision, not the deed.
  Greatness is to be one with the vision, and ensue it,
  greatness is suffering, greatness a long need,
  and distant bugles crying faintly through it,
        " Lights out! Lights out! "
  Greatness is to hear the bugles and not to doubt.

But loud these bugles for the doer cry,
    and the sound of his longing for beauty is dim,
    as note after note ascends his evening sky,
    stealing the ancient stars and the moon from him,
        to range instead
    the frozen constellations of the vision fled.

And the great man's greatness marches by his side,
    fainter with the rising bugles on the air,
    as though the whole world were a voice that cried,
    " To-day and here, not then nor over there,"
        and no great lily
    of the trump of vision at dawn will sound réveillé.

And thus the uncommon man is Lucifer
    falling in his own heart, so hidden at birth
    with the great wings of vision, so far from her
    wandered with the green laurels of the earth,
        so standing, crowned
    by men, hears the wings pass until there is no sound.

" These lost the world.   These are lost archangels."
    Whence came these words?   Not in my mind they
        rose,
    but strangely stirred, as though green-brazen bells
    were rubbed by fingers, lighter than the snows,
        so faint with such
    far cry of bronze beneath a cold and feathery touch.

Who are the losers of the world?   Not those
    millions, whose spark is blown upon the wind,
    to make one petal of the fiery rose
    which they, who nurse their flame, can never find,
        not those who spend,
    and lay their beauty down for their unknown friend.
102

Who are the lost archangels?   Not the gentle
   who are as rich as the blades of grass, that stand
   content to be one thread in the green mantle
   in which spring enters on Broceliande,
         not those who give
   their lives that greater lives than theirs may live.

We lose the world.   We are lost archangels,
   who take their gift, and, taking, lose our own,
   we the magicians weaker than our spells,
   the lesser sculptors than the patient stone,
         we, who by this
   are given all loveliness to fashion, and to miss.

We lose the world.   And yet, in losing, see
   by their lost sight, feel by their wasted touch,
   and find the face of God bewilderingly,
   because these others loved their dream too much,
         because we love it
   too little, and through them become the meaning of it.

We are the losers of the world, and we have it.
   We are the lost archangels, and we rise.
   We have cheated the faith they had, and they forgave
      it,
   blind, and we see behind their darkened eyes.
         Died, and instead
   are the life eternal for which all these are dead.

I

THE FEATHERS in a fan
are not so frail as man;
the green embosséd leaf
than man is no more brief.
His life is not so loud
as the passing of a cloud;
his death is quieter
than harebells, when they stir.
The years that have no form
and substance are as warm,
and space has hardly less
supreme an emptiness.
And yet man being frail
does on himself prevail,
and with a single thought
can bring the world to naught,
as being brief he still
bends to his fleeting will
all time, and makes of it
the shadow of his wit.
Soundless in life and death
although he vanisheth,
the echo of a song
makes all the stars a gong.
Cold, void, and yet the grim
darkness is hot with him,
and space is but the span
of the long love of man.

II

THE CROSS was but the iron clamps that hold
    the shutter at a window.   Slip the bars
and, with a rush, come flooding in, all gold,
    the tides of day, or evening with her stars.
But say He had not touched the shutter, say
    He'd waited in the darkness patiently,
and suffered all life long, day after day,
    his slow habitual Gethsemane.
God, the old Pharaoh, obstinate and blind,
    rubbed by that gradual proof of all men's woe,
might at the last have understood mankind,
    and for His own sake let His people go,
and the Crucified become the Crucifying,
if Christ had lived for men instead of dying.

THE UNCOMMON WOMAN

I LEAN back through the dark forest of my race,
    and all the floor is heaped with delicate ash
    of leaf and blossom, and husk too small to trace—
    all that is left of man's imperious flesh
        made manifest
    in battle, love, and the journey to the Islands of the
      West.

Not his these scented ashes, this bland air,
    but Nature's only, muttering in her sleep,
    " Let life go on," and does not know nor care
    if all who live are foundered fathoms deep,
        like sinking wrack
    changing from gold to green, from green to unim-
    agined black.

Old wars, the desperate bid for life by dying,
    mix with dust Edens long ago forgotten,
    and here Gethsemanes in ash are lying
    browner than last year's leaves, as those leaves
    rotten,
        all nature's tricks—
    even the last sweet treachery of a Crucifix.

But woman has a secret that resists
    the magic of the half-gods, as they wind
    their spells with slow, but surely wearying, wrists,
    woman has a secret not all their webs can bind—
        the little Powers
    weaving for their own necks these sacrificial flowers.

What is our secret, Eve?   When the coiled snake
    tempts us with knowledge, and we whisper " Yes "?
What is our secret, Mary?   When they take
our dream and crucify it? and no less
            we must outdream
    the serpent-trick of knowledge, and man's blind
        stratagem?

What is the secret of women, that jettison
    the Edens that they have for spectral gleams
    of impossible Edens always further on?
    Who offer up the child Jesus of their dreams
            to the sharp nails,
    that hammer into Hell the broken dream that fails?

What is their secret?   Woman is older than man,
    and is not cheated by the manifold pretence
    of life that has no purpose and no plan,
    wooing with spring and flowers and trees the sense
            of those, who should
    look into darkness in cold undecorated solitude.

Woman, that bears, has a higher fate than bearing.
    Woman, that gives, outlasts both giving and taking.
    Woman, that loves, outloves the need of caring.
    Woman, that dies, is moulding death, forsaking
            life's fleeting guesses
    for the rich dark, and sempiternal lovelinesses.

She is the labyrinth that man has trod
  led by the tapes of love the conjurer,
  who in that guidance dreams himself a god,
  and does not guess that in the heart of her
      he is no more
  than, gazing over seas unknown, the Minotaur.

She is the constant in the bewildering flow
  of numbers, written in chalk on death's long slate,
  to which death has the key, but does not know
  how that one figure, stronger far than fate,
      will crash the sum
  in the gold total of her proud Kingdom Come.

And the Uncommon Woman, whatever shape
  man's wandering fancy gives her, Ashtaroth,
  Psyche, or Eve or Mary, cannot escape
  from that in men and women, transcending both
      the primal trust,
  to which she is appointed, of the patient dust,

twisted and battered, suffering and torn,
  but clamouring ever through its shapeless mouth
  for sheerer peaks than thought's last Matterhorn,
  for swallow-flights past beauty's furthest South,
      for that which must
  be the whole meaning of dust, because it is not dust.

To that all women are pledged, and do not know it,
  and I, the uncommon woman, who dimly see
  that we are the first conjecture of a poet,
  one line in an unconcerted harmony,
      I will not falter,
  myself the flame, I shall not see, upon the unseen
  altar.

I

WHEN the ancient ape and fish
mould man's spirit to their wish,
when the battle in the brain,
fought and won, is lost again,
when in fear or hate or rage
man disowns his heritage,
when the heart's imagining
plucks the angel by the wing,
and at the first defiling touch
the great white pinions wheel and clutch,
clutch and wheel, and with one great
impulse leave man desolate,
what remains?   What prayer, what priest
can stay the empire of the beast?
What new legions can be hurled
into the breach to save the world?
But stay! a lantern in the dark,
and in the night a bugle, hark!
Have hope, my spirit!   There appears
down the dark victorious years,
where man has fallen, cool and slim,
the captain God aneled for him.
Her beauty is the clarion
of the new armies sweeping on,
the trumpet-note whose echoes spill
from darkened hill to darkened hill.
And where the broken hosts have reeled
she lifts her courage like a shield,
lifts up her laughter like a sword,
and flings them back, released, restored,
bursting the ultimate night apart
with the artillery of her heart,
and, where the scattered clouds were piled,
bearing the morning, like a child.

II

I AM the spring of tree and flower and beast,
   in man's wild blood my settled pulses stir,
and, while his sun still modifies the East
   with his blonde torch, I am his prisoner.
But tree and flower and beast are only a name
   for man's brief dreams, and even the sun is naught,
with all his lenient planets, but a flame
   that blazes, and will perish, in a thought.
And till these pass, the secret in me trembles,
   waiting its hour, and still I keep between
the half-seen truth, of which all these are symbols,
   and the whole truth, where sight is one with seen,
where even love lays by man's last pretence
of consummation in difference.

LOSERS AND WINNERS

I. THE LOSERS

We lost the world.   We are lost archangels
and time abandons us, and we become
the silence in heaven when no organ swells
between the stars, and even the moon is dumb—
     we sons and daughters
of light are darkness on the face of the waters,

dark with the flame, whose plume is black in Hell,
at which the angels of despair are lit,
Lucifer, who fell with Adam, and Azrael,
and, deeply burning in the heart of it,
     how can they save
when our pale spirits call them from a nameless
grave?

We lost the world.   We are not even weary,
passing beyond despair and comfort both,
and, if our hands are spoiled, could you, pale Mary,
restore them, or our hearts, you, Ashtaroth?
     Can you not save,
Mary and Ashtaroth, nor hear us in the grave?

We rose like archangels, and afterward
through cycle after flaming epicycle
in the doomed armies lift a broken sword
to share that doom, but you remember, Michael,
     that, if they name us,
we, dying, praised the " morituri salutamus,"

113

and that long cry, if even our names are lost,
    may echo through the frozen festival,
    where what we might have been—a silent host
    of cold spectators—sees us fight and fall,
            but if we come,
    their own ghosts crying, who will dare to turn the
        thumb?

We lost the world, soldier and prostitute,
    the common man and woman of despair,
    who play on life as on a ruined flute
    when nothing but the will to play is there,
            and our poor breath
    has only the two stops, false life and falser death.

We are lost archangels.   You, Magdalene,
    since you, like us, the source of life had marred
    in death's dull cause, had it not better been
    rather these heads to anoint with spikenard,
            these bent, these grey,
    for whom there are no angels to roll the stone away?

For whom there is no archangel to plead
    in heaven, or advance their case in hell,
    who buy from Lucifer with bitter need
    oblivion in the dark of Azrael,
            and who must sell,
    hucksters, the freedom for which the angels fell?

Is there no archangel, no spirit lief
    to save the huckster that all men may be?
    None?   But, bright choir, there was once a thief

who found his archangel on Calvary—
    a thief who won
by his acceptance the life rejected by the nun,

the cloistered nun who laid the world aside
    before the world had spoken, and no less
    in all of us is man's unsatisfied
    desire for more than human holiness
        in the heart spared
(Who knows?) because of the agony of love it shared.

The unknown love to which we sacrificed,
    destroying other gods, and clove to this,
    an older Mithras and a darker Christ,
    and yet betrayed him with the Judas-kiss
        to those who saw
through lawlessness only the cold avenging law,

who would not see that to defy the rule,
    through it destroy the law, builds it anew
    out of rebellion more beautiful
    than the old law that custom made untrue,
        who sacrificed
for that bleak satisfaction even Christ.

And therefore, Archangels, since you are jealous
    guardians in heaven of the source of love,
    lean down from your high sanctuary and tell us,
    while still upon our souls the shadows move,
        we shall not starve
in heaven, on earth who only stand and serve.

We lost the world.   Fall with us, Lucifer!
Cover us with your darkness, Azrael!
We are lost archangels.   Then cry to her,
to Mary, with your trumpeters in Hell,
     Michael, and say,
" But these have found the world, who laid the world
away."

And Mary Mother, to whom this much was given,
dream like the rest, and, like the rest, outdreaming
this dream of life, remember these in heaven,
and in that world where there's an end of seeming,
     for all these dead,
Mary, be comfortable for the uncomforted.

II. THE WINNERS

We won the world.   We are the victors!   Yes,
all that it has to offer, we shall use it—
love, power, beauty, wisdom, holiness,
we have the world, and having it must lose it,
     for only thus
can He, Who made us to conquer, with pity conquer
us.

And Love is Lucifer and Azrael,
Mary, who, having much, had this more given.
Michael and Mary Magdalene of Hell
building with separate agonies the heaven,
     cool, fair and far,
that rises steadily in a single star,

seen from the abyss of life, where fear and hate
through loss, and suffering, and faith reclaim
the love their failure proves, and consecrate
the tossing veils of vision with the same
beauty that died,
and rose again, when the world's heart was crucified.

The same that all must know, when the wings beating
draw up the heart, that saw in a glass darkly
into an alien star to the last meeting,
when between wings the wingless heart sees starkly,
in the disgrace
of love that falls so short of Him, God face to face.

Love, that falls short, even the love creating
the figment of His beauty in the soul,
where beast and angel each on other waiting
are, though divided, thus for ever whole,
and each in each
grope back to the jungle, and up to heaven reach.

As all who teach, building with human stuff
as the builder with the earth, can never rest
nor find the beauty they fashion is enough
beside the one unfashionable best,
whose golden strands
escape their hands for ever, and are not made with
hands.

They mould a Saviour, but they cannot save him,
nor save themselves by his star-fated loss,
and life does not forgive though they forgave him,

117

manhood's surrender weeping on the Cross,
" Why did you waken me
to light, if thus in dark you have forsaken me? "

Nor even the Saints of victory claim more
than to endure defeat without complaint,
and the failure of the crowns they battled for,
and not the crowns they gathered, seal the saint,
for the heart knows
that the secret of sainthood is complex as the rose,

plotted in long conspiracy of pain,
moulded with the moon, and with the sun's gold
hands,
whispered by snow, and hinted at by rain,
guessed in wild forests in forgotten lands,
in leaves, like a devil,
and flowers like angry flames that predicated evil,

until a poet by some half-fabled city,
under the moon on turrets fairy-pale,
saw, with the anguish of love that melts to pity
for all perfection that is born to fail,
in darkness climb
the first consummate rose from beauty into time.

And sainthood is as old as the rose and as rich
with history of anguish, and the thorn
of Time bewildering the hush, in which
the flower of eternity is born,
and the dark advances
where you are burning, Joan, and where you pray,
St. Francis.

And yet, dear Saints, if all things mortal must
    be dull with earth, and with the darkness faint,
    mortality is canonized with dust,
    and the dark it suffers anoints the heart a saint,
        and man's desire
failing in heaven is fire that speaks to fire.

Thus lovers, Builder, teacher, and the Saint,
    the uncommon man and woman, glory gain
    to find their little victories grow faint,
    and all their battles to be fought again,
        and never can
do more than prove for the common woman and man,

that woman, who bears, has a higher fate than bearing,
    woman, that gives, outlasts both giving and taking,
    woman, that loves, outloves the need of caring,
    and woman, that fails, is of her failure making
        the only guess
of our brief hearts at sempiternal loveliness,

that these are the losers of the world, and they have it,
    they are the lost archangels, and they rise,
    they have cheated the faith they had, and God for-
      gave it,
    are blind and see in His forgiving eyes,
        and, having died,
of life eternal are the bridegroom and the bride.

CODA

THE HIGH song is over.   Silent is the lute now.
  They are crowned for ever and discrowned now.
Whether they triumphed or suffered they are mute now,
  or at the most they are only a sound now.

The high song is over.   There is none to complain now.
  No heart for healing, and none to break now.
They have gone, and they will not come again now.
  They are sleeping at last, and they will not wake
    now.

The high song is over.   And we shall not mourn now.
  There was a thing to say, and it is said now.
It is as though all these had been unborn now,
  it is as though the world itself were dead now.

The high song is over.   Even the echoes fail now;
  winners and losers—they are only a theme now,
their victory and defeat a half-forgotten tale now;
  and even the angels are only a dream now.

There is no need for blame, no cause for praise now.
  Nothing to hide, to change or to discover.
They were men and women.   They have gone their
    ways now,
  as men and women must.   The high song is over.

R. Clay & Sons, Ltd., Bungay, Suffolk.